Let's Look! Nurse Shark

An Up-Close Look at Habitat

by Chelsea Donaldson

Photo Credits: t = top, b = bottom, l = left, r = right, c = center

Front Cover: Stephen Frink/Corbis Images; 1: frantisekhojdysz/Shutterstock; 2–3: Carlos Villoch/Alamy; 2tr: Jurgen Freund/Nature Picture Library; 3br: Jolanta Wojcicka/Shutterstock; 4–5: Matt9122/Shutterstock; 5cl: Nikita Tiunov/Shutterstock; 5cc: Sean Lema/Shutterstock; 5cr: Durden Images/Shutterstock; 5br: frantisekhojdysz/Shutterstock; 6–7: WaterFrame/Alamy; 7br: WaterFrame/Alamy; 8–9: Shane Gross/Shutterstock; 9br: Michael Rothschild/Shutterstock; 10–11: Chris & Monique Fallows/Nature Picture Library; 11br: Jeffrey L. Rotman/Corbis; 12–13: Darren J. Bradley/Shutterstock; 12c: Norbert Wu/National Geographic; 14–15: Greg Amptman/Shutterstock; 14cl: Jolanta Wojcicka/Shutterstock; 14cr: frantisekhojdysz/Shutterstock; 15tl: WaterFrame/Alamy; 15tr: Michael Rothschild/Shutterstock; 15bc: Jeffrey L. Rotman/Corbis Images; 16: Michele Westmorland/Corbis Images; Back Cover: frantisekhojdysz/Shutterstock.

Developed and Produced by Focus Strategic Communications, Inc.
Design and Layout by Rob Scanlan
Photo Research by Karen Hunter
Photo Edit by Cynthia Carris
Illustrations by Deborah Crowle

978-0-545-75174-2

12 11 10 9 8 7 6 5 4 3 2 1   14 15 16 17 18/0

Printed in the U.S.A.   40

First printing, September 2014

Let's look at the nurse shark!

Do you like to play hide-and-seek?
So do nurse sharks!

2

They like to hide in shallow, sandy areas.
Nurse sharks live in groups on the
bottom of the ocean.

Let's look at their habitat.

Nurse sharks live in warm, shallow waters.
Some live in **coral reefs**.
Most nurse sharks like to stay in the same place all day.

Coral reefs are also home to many small creatures. Nurse sharks can find lots to eat here.

shrimp crab mollusk

Let's look at hunting.

Nurse sharks are not fast swimmers or fierce hunters. They hunt at night, when their **prey** is asleep!

But nurse sharks face other dangers.
People!

Let's look at human threats.

People make nets for catching fish to eat.
People don't eat nurse sharks.
But sometimes a shark gets caught in these nets.

People also **pollute** the water.
Dirty water can hurt coral reefs.
This makes it hard for nurse sharks
to find food and hide from predators.

We must take care of our oceans.
Then the nurse sharks will keep swimming,
sleeping, and eating!

Let's look at what we have learned about nurse sharks.

The nurse shark:

lives in warm, shallow waters

hunts shrimp, crabs, and other small creatures

leaves its mother as
soon as it is born

sometimes gets eaten
by other sharks

can be hurt by people

Nurse sharks are full of surprises!

GLOSSARY

coral reef   an ocean habitat created by coral where nurse sharks like to live

habitat   the natural world that an animal or plant lives in

human threats   things that people do that are dangerous to other creatures, like pollute

hunting   searching for prey

pollute   to put something into the water, soil, or air that is dirty and can cause harm

predator   an animal that eats another animal

prey   an animal that is food to another animal

pup   a baby shark